~~Who Am I?~~

Who Does God Say I Am?

Breanna Williams

This book is dedicated to my mother, JoAnn Gulley, and brother, Stephen "Dion" Williams Jr. Thank you for your encouragement and support.

Love, Bree

A Friendly Reminder Before

You Begin

I understand that you might feel this page isn't necessary, but I kindly ask for a moment of your time.

Can you take a deep breath, set aside any preconceived notions, and open your heart to what God has in store for you? You're entering a welcoming space where you can listen, observe, receive, and reflect. There's no right or wrong—only opportunities for growth.

So, I invite you to take a moment to reflect and appreciate where you are, and let's embark on this journey together.

Let's begin!

The Sign You're Looking For

Is People

"God, send me a sign."

I've noticed that God's signs or messages often come through people. The Bible provides numerous examples, such as the many prophets God sent to teach, deliver, and warn the children of Israel.

Mordecai assisted Esther by providing her with information and mentoring her on how to approach the king to save her people (Esther 4).

Jonathan helped David escape from his father, King Saul (1 Samuel 20).

John the Baptist was sent to prepare the way for Christ (Isaiah 40:3; Matthew 3:3).

Mary Magdalene was sent to inform the Apostles that Christ had risen (John 20:11-18).

~~Who Am I?~~ Who Does God Say I Am?

Peter was sent to Cornelius, Philip to the Ethiopian Eunuch, and Ananias to Saul, who later became Paul (Acts 10; Acts 8:26-40; Acts 9:10-19).

Ask God for discernment and guidance on recognizing the helpers He is sending you. Life is too overwhelming to handle alone, and the great news is that you don't have to. I would not be as knowledgeable, confident, and grounded as I am today if it weren't for the messengers God has sent my way.

Thank you for giving me life and teaching me to recognize that I am a King's Kid!

Your Reflection

{ Could you pause for a moment and journey back in time? Who were the people who walked alongside you, offering their support and guidance?

{ Who has He sent recently?

{ I understand that your current circumstances may not be ideal, but can we both acknowledge the profound impact of these helping hands in our lives?

{ God uses us to help others.

{ You don't have to do it alone.

_____

_____

_____

_____

_____

_____

_____

~~Who Am I?~~ Who Does God Say I Am?

_____

_____

_____

_____

_____

_____

_____

_____

_____

_____

_____

_____

Breanna Williams

Your Perception Of The Father

I am speaking from my experience, and you may feel the same.

How I viewed God made it difficult to accept and trust Him. My perception of God was that He was an old man with a long beard sitting on the throne and watching my every move. Each and every time I made a mistake:

Zap! (Consequence)

Zap!

Zap!

But when I finally met Him face to face and sat at his feet, I realized how loving and concerned He really was about me.

The zaps I called consequences were not precisely from God; they were the reaping of seeds I had sown. For example, I entered into a relationship with a guy who literally told me that he did not love himself. As a result, he treated me poorly (true story).

Father never wanted that for me because He literally teaches us what a healthy marriage should look like (Matthew 22:34-40; Ephesians 5:28-33).

Another reason I had a difficult time trusting God was that I did not understand how it felt to have a loving father. My dad had not been part of my life, and trying to see God as my dad was not happening.

As you continue discovering how God describes you, you will see how important you are to Him and how much He really loves you.

My relationship went from calling Him:

God

Father

Dad

Daddy

Dada (Abba, Romans 8:15)

He is my Dada. And it has been the best daddy-daughter relationship I've ever had.

Your Reflection

{ How do you see God?

{ What is your perception of the Father?

_____

_____

_____

_____

_____

_____

_____

_____

Breanna Williams

"*Who Am I?*"

It's quite a common question, and you'd be surprised that many people struggle to answer it.

When someone says, "Tell us about yourself," you might feel inclined to list your occupation, marital status, parental status, age, educational qualifications, place of origin, and hobbies.

For instance, you may say, "I grew up in Arkansas and served in the Navy for twelve years. I am a teacher, a published author, and a podcast host. My husband's name is James, and we have two boys, Jamie and Bryan. I enjoy hiking, learning new things, and trying out different cuisines. My favorite food is sushi."

Sound familiar?

It is the cookie-cutter introduction we all use to begin a good conversation.

But . . . is that who you truly are?

Many of us spent years in college, retired from the military, and have multiple titles and initials before and after our names. We have years of experience, success, money, and a family, yet we still suffer from deep sadness and a void.

A void that no matter what you do, you can never fill.

And that void is not knowing who we are. Not having an answer to "Who am I?" Being confused between what people see or say about you and what you believe about yourself.

Identity is what you "believe" about yourself.

So, what or who is sourcing your beliefs?

My identity was attached to the twelve years of blood, sweat, and tears I spent building a successful career in the Navy. I navigated warships, among other impressive things; I was a subject-matter expert, led teams, prevented and fixed problems, and was dependable. I had elevated through the ranks, overcome many challenges, and made a name for myself.

But when I really think about it, my identity was not my title. It was my perseverance, my will to never give up, my grit, my fight, my strength, and my pride, never to let them see me cry.

But where did the idea of never letting them see me cry originate? Why did I believe I had to be so strong? Without words, it was taught to me through the women in my life because they had no choice but to be strong.

I learned from their experience and told myself, "No one is coming to help you. If you want it done right, you must do it yourself."

Hearing those statements and seeing them played out over and over again until my soul adopted them and seared them into my being. I learned it was me against the world.

I graduated high school in May and was in boot camp in August 2009. Immediately realizing the life I chose was not for the weak at heart, I added layers of skin throughout the years and tons of emotional weight. Not to bore you with all the details, but my Navy career sucked! What I thought was strength was really fear, and I had no place to express it because everyone around me suffered from the same illness and was in the same position: suffering in silence, calling it strength and calling it normal.

My last two years in the Navy were the worst, and I broke. They say that you know when it's time to separate from the military. I tapped out at eleven years and only stayed for twelve years and two months because I had to complete the time on my contract. Eleven years. During the remaining twelve months, I was army-crawling through hell to reach the finish line.

I hated my life. But at least I was being paid, right? Money was more than oxygen to me because I saw and understood the feeling of financial struggles, and it tore a hole of insecurities within me. Being financially sound gave me comfort and pride, especially being able to help my family, which gave me even more surety and confidence in who I was.

I was *Ms. Fix-It*. When people had an issue, they came to me. When someone needed advice, I helped them even when they did not ask for my help. Problems were like puzzles I had to put together. I prided myself on fixing my problems, fighting my battles, and providing for myself. I rarely, very seldomly, asked for help because I didn't want to be a bother. But more honestly, when I asked for help, I didn't get it, which confirmed my beliefs even more that I had to do everything for myself.

Hearing statements like, "Oh, Breanna got it," "Go ask Williams," and "I can always rely on you" made it even more challenging to admit that I needed help. I suffered in silence until I fixed my problems and carried on as I was taught to - **a proud, independent black woman.**

But still, something was missing.

Religion and family were triggers because I had different views. My religion did not make sense to me. I was that kid with 1,001 questions and was never afraid to ask. But as I grew older, I realized my questions were never answered; teachers only danced around them in hopes I would just let it go and follow suit. So, I pretended for as long as possible and obeyed because I did not want to go to hell. But after a while, I broke and stopped believing in God and religion altogether. I felt at ease. But I felt judged by others when I told them I did not go to church or believe in all that stuff. But still at ease. Good and bad things happen. That is just the way life is. If you work hard and treat people right, you will succeed.

But still, something was missing.

I finally had a fantastic relationship, or so I thought. Marriage, traveling, babies, and growing old together were the topics. We were making plans for the future, and I was so happy because I had finally met the love of my life!

Yes, Lord!

But.

Underneath it all, it wasn't fantastic. I was sad. I worked hard to make it work. I changed this, and I did that, but nothing was working.

I can't have another failed relationship. I'm thirty-one.

Maybe I'm overreacting.

I'm in my head again; just let it flow.

When I separated from the Navy, I started a business, worked really hard, treated people right, and became profitable. I understood the risks, so I did what I always did: prepare for the worst. Ms. Fix-It understood that preparation was key. Before separating, I had significant savings and stocks, and of course, if I worked as hard as I did in the Navy for myself, I would surely succeed!

But after a while, the risks became struggles.

My finances were depleted faster than I was making money, and I could no longer help my family and, in many cases, help myself.

Okay, it's time to find a job. I'm a Navy veteran with tons of experience, and employers will love to have me.

Job application after job application. Job interview after job interview. I even applied to fast food and the Family Dollar store, and they said no.

Wait! I mean, come on!

I worked so hard. I was a good person. I treated others right. But I was failing! Why could I not fix it? I thought I was better than this!

I was told that the reason I wasn't winning in life was that my identity was not aligned with my goals.

Hmmm. So, how do I change my identity? What do I need to change?

Who am I, really?

The sad part is the person who told me that did not know how to help me because they had not learned who they were. But one thing is true: God uses everything and everyone.

I read books, listened to podcasts, and still wrestled with not finding the answer until the moment I heard,

You're asking the wrong person who you are. Instead, who does God say you are?

I asked people and myself instead of the Creator, God.

I am a creation asking other creations who I am, seeking validation. My job, boss, family, friends, boyfriend, strength, and wisdom were all imperfect, fleeting, and misleading.

It's like asking my Nike how to repair my iPhone instead of going to the creator.

Instead, why not ask God, "Who am I?"

Ask, and it will be given to you; seek and you will find; knock and the door will be opened to you. For everyone who asks receives; and the one who seeks finds; and to the one who knocks, the door will be opened.

—Matthew 7:7-8

~~Who Am I?~~ Who Does God Say I Am?

Let's take a journey to learn who God is and who you are to Him.

Attached to each scripture is an I AM statement. Throughout the day, meditate on the statement along with the scripture. How do you feel? What ideas have you come across? What are your thoughts?

Take your time. Analyze the scripture and your thoughts. Invite the Holy Spirit to provide revelation and understanding.

Your Reflection

{ What is your current identity?

{ What do you believe about yourself?

{ Why do you believe that about yourself?

{ What are your beliefs anchored in?

{ What do you want to change, and what would you like to remain the same?

_____

_____

_____

_____

_____

_____

_____

_____

~~Who Am I?~~ Who Does God Say I Am?

_____

_____

_____

_____

_____

_____

_____

_____

_____

_____

_____

Genesis 1:1

In the beginning, God created the heavens and

the earth.

God Is The Alpha And The

Omega

The first point I found was:

"In the beginning, God . . ."

The very first subject we are introduced to is God.

My first instinct was to look to others for help, advice, guidance, and love. When that failed, I looked inward to provide for myself, but drawing from a dry well was impossible. When I have nothing else to give, then what?

My parents know a lot more about many things because they were here before me. They are old! However, how old is God? He was here before either of us, meaning He knows all. So, when I and others failed, God held and cared for me through it all.

He was there during the many days I felt alone and out of place.

He was there when I thought there was no more road to travel; He was the source.

And if they did help me, they were only helping because God was helping them to help me. They, too, were relying on God.

God is the beginning.

He is the beginning of everything and everyone.

Genesis 1:3

And God said, "Let there be light," and there

was light.

God Is The Creator

The second point of Genesis 1:1 is, what does God do? He creates.

> *In the beginning, God created the heaven and the earth.*
>
> —Genesis 1:1

> *And God said, Let there be light, and there was light.*
>
> —Genesis 1:3

> *And God said, "Let there be a space between the waters, to separate the waters of the heavens from the waters of the heavens from the earth. And that is what happened. God made this space to separate the waters of the earth from the waters of the heavens.*

God called the space "sky."
—Genesis 1:6-8

One way, God reveals himself to us through his creations (Romans 1:20).

Everything we see as new is a "discovery" was already here, for there is nothing new under the sun (Ecclesiastes 1:9-11).

However, out of all the wonders in the world, we humans are his most loved creations, and out of all the humans, he knows my name and cares for me individually (Matthew 6:26-27, John 10:3)

Genesis 1:26

Then God said, "Let us make mankind in our image, in our likeness, so that they may rule over the fish in the sea and the birds in the sky, over the livestock and all the wild animals, and over all the creatures that move along the ground."

I Am Made In God's Image

And Likeness

I want to share something that truly resonates with me: so many times, I overlook the profound truth that I am an image of God—a reflection of my Father. He created me to resemble Him!

When I gaze into the mirror, I see more than just my own reflection; I see God staring back at me.

When others meet me, there's a unique opportunity for them to glimpse God through my existence. And the same applies when they see you—you reflect God, too.

It's much like the bond between siblings. Each child carries their own distinct features, yet they all reflect their parents in beautiful ways. Each individual shines with the essence and personality of their parents, and similarly, God has bestowed upon us His own likeness and pieces of His personality.

Isn't that truly amazing? You are deeply loved, for He intentionally designed you to mirror Him, showcasing your own unique beauty in the world.

Your Reflection

{ What comes to mind when you read that God is the beginning?

{ What does it mean, to you, to be made in the likeness and image of God?

{ How do you feel when learning that God gave you His DNA by breathing into your lungs?

{ What feelings do you have about that?

{ Where are those feelings coming from?

{ What ideas, beliefs, or teachings question this to be true?

{ Are you beginning to see how important you are to God?

_____

_____

_____

Breanna Williams

~~Who Am I?~~ Who Does God Say I Am?

_____

_____

_____

_____

_____

_____

_____

_____

_____

_____

Genesis 2:7

Then the Lord God formed a man from the dust of the ground and breathed into his nostrils the breath of life, and the man became a living being.

God Is My Father

Not only did God create me in His image and likeness, but He also gave me His DNA.

He loves humans more than any other creation.

I am a part of God.

God is my Father.

Breanna Williams

Genesis 2:25

Adam and his wife were both naked, and they felt no shame.

I Am Created To Be

Unashamed

We often use shame and guilt interchangeably, but they are different. Shame is feeling embarrassed or humiliated because of a choice or decision. In contrast, guilt is feeling sorry for a mistake that causes others discomfort.

You see, guilt focuses on the action, and shame focuses on the self.

As noted in the verse above, Adam and Eve were completely comfortable naked. They did not even know the meaning of nakedness or shame because it was not God's intention for us to experience it.

And he said, "Who told you that you were naked?

Have you eaten from the tree that I commanded

you not to eat from?"

—Genesis 3:11 (NIV)

For the Spirit God gave us does not make us timid, but gives us power, love and self-discipline.

—2 Timothy 1:7 (NIV)

For God is not the author of confusion but of peace, as in all the churches of the saints.

—1 Corinthians 14:33 (NKJV)

So, where do you believe shame came from if God did not create His children to experience it?

And he said, "Who told you that you were naked?
Have you eaten from the tree that I commanded
you not to eat from?"
—Genesis 3:11 (NIV)

Then the Lord God said to the woman, "What is
this you have done?" The woman said, "The
serpent deceived me, and I ate." So the Lord God
said to the serpent, "Because you have done this,
'Cursed are you above all livestock and all wild
animals! You will crawl on your belly and you will
eat dust all the days of your life.'"
—Genesis 3:13-14 (NIV)

But why did Eve eat from the tree?

"You will not certainly die," the serpent said to the woman. "For God knows that when you eat from it your eyes will be opened, and you will be like God, knowing good and evil."

—Genesis 3:4-5 (NIV)

Hmm, wasn't Eve already like God? He created her in His image and breathed life into her (Genesis 2:7). He also cared for her and spent time with her (Genesis 2:9; Genesis 3:8). However, Satan caused Eve to question her identity in God, making her feel like she was lacking something or that God was withholding information.

He employs a similar tactic against Jesus in Matthew 4:1-11.

"If you are the Son of God . . ."

-Matthew 4:2

"If you are the Son of God . . ."

~~Who Am I?~~ Who Does God Say I Am?

-Matthew 4:6

"All of this I will give you . . ."

-Matthew 4:9

Satan tries to prompt Christ to doubt His status as the Son and make Him believe He lacks something or that God is withholding information from Him.

However, Christ knew who He was in God!

Your Reflection

{ What are you currently ashamed of?

{ How has Satan made you question your identity in God?

{ What has been said to make you feel less than a child of God?

{ What will it take to have confidence in your identity in Christ?

_____

_____

_____

_____

_____

~~Who Am I?~~ Who Does God Say I Am?

_____

_____

_____

_____

_____

_____

_____

_____

_____

_____

_____

_____

Psalms 139:13-16

For you created my inmost being; you knit me together in my mother's womb.

I praise you because I am fearfully and wonderfully made; your works are wonderful, I know that full well.

My frame was not hidden from you when I was made in the secret place, when I was woven together in the depths of the earth.

Your eyes saw my unformed body; all the days ordained for me were written in your book before one of them came to be.

Luke 12:7

Indeed, the very hairs of your head are all numbered. Don't be afraid; you are worth more than many sparrows.

I AM FEARFULLY AND WONDERFULLY MADE.

I AM KNOWN BY GOD.

I AM MADE WITH A PURPOSE.

Father, God knew me even before I was conceived!

Do you realize that science cannot fully understand the divine mystery of conception without God's involvement? Babies may arrive at a different time than expected. Moreover, no one knows how a baby will look and sound or what their personality will be like. But God knows! God crafted you in your mother's womb. He understood you intimately before your parents even knew you existed. He established your purpose before your birth.

There's nothing you can hide from Him, nor can you catch Him by surprise. Thus, instead of trying to determine this alone, wouldn't it be wiser to ask God what His purpose is for you?

Jeremiah 1:5-8

Before I formed you in the womb I knew you, before you were born I set you apart; I appointed you as a prophet to the nations.

Alas, Sovereign Lord," I said, "I do not know how to speak; I am too young.

But the Lord said to me, "Do not say, 'I am too young.' You must go to everyone I send you and say whatever I command you. Do not be afraid of them, for I am with you and will rescue you," declares the Lord.

I AM GIVEN A PURPOSE.

I AM PREPARED.

Have you noticed that each person God calls on feels unprepared and reluctant to fulfill their purpose?

God replies, saying, *I am with you. I will tell you what to say. I will protect you. I will provide for you. All you have to do is believe and go.*

I realized that I sometimes felt unqualified for certain tasks, so I decided to set them aside. However, when it's a divine calling, the mission reemerges; I can't overlook it.

I once came across the saying, "God doesn't call the qualified"; he qualifies the called, which truly unsettled me! Nevertheless, there's an element of truth in it. Initially, I might not feel equipped, but as I persist in my faith, I acquire knowledge, enhance my skills, and ultimately accomplish the mission.

Your Reflection

{ What revelations came to you when you read those scriptures?

{ How do you feel knowing God knitted you in your mother's womb?

{ How do you feel knowing that he wrote your story before you were conceived?

{ Does it feel like an honor or a challenge?

{ Do you see how important you are to God?

_____

_____

_____

_____

_____

_____

~~Who Am I?~~ Who Does God Say I Am?

_____

_____

_____

_____

_____

_____

_____

_____

_____

_____

_____

_____

Breanna Williams

Genesis 1:26

Then God said, "Let us make mankind in our image, in our

likeness, so that they may rule over the fish in the sea and

the birds in the sky, over the livestock and all the wild

animals, and over all the creatures that move along the

ground."

Breanna Williams

I Am Above All Of God's

Creations

We are captivated by the beauty and majesty of lions, cheetahs, elephants, and, of course, our cats and dogs. We shouldn't overlook the stunning vistas of the ocean and mountains, as well as the intricate designs of flowers and plants.

God, the creator of all, holds a special and deep love for you. You are His most treasured creation, made in His image. He values you above all other beings and cares for you in a uniquely profound way.

Look at the birds of the air; they do not sow or reap or store away in barns, and yet your

Heavenly Father feeds them. Are you not much more valuable than they?

—Matthew 6:26

Did Christ die for you or the animals?

You are the center of God's creations.

You are the apple of His eye (Psalms 17:8).

Bask in His Love for you!

Your Reflection

{ You hold greater importance than any animals or creations. His love for you is so profound that Christ sacrificed Himself for your sins and shortcomings. Every mistake you've made and will make in the future has been addressed by Christ on the cross. No other creation has received such unconditional love from God.

{ What emotions are you experiencing right now?

_____

_____

_____

_____

_____

~~Who Am I?~~ Who Does God Say I Am?

_____

_____

_____

_____

_____

_____

_____

_____

_____

_____

_____

_____

Breanna Williams

Matthew 6:25

"Therefore I tell you, do not worry about your life, what you will eat or drink; or about your body, what you will wear. Is not life more than food, and the body more than clothes?"

Ephesians 1:4

For he chose us in him before the creation of the world to be

holy and blameless in his sight.

I Am Chosen

From the very beginning, you were chosen. You were part of God's plan all along, as He created everything for you.

When God created Adam and Eve, they were innocent, free from sin, shame, or guilt. Genesis 2:25 states that Adam and his wife were both naked and felt no shame. Yes, you may make mistakes. However, remember that through Christ's sacrifice, you are forgiven.

No matter how serious you think your errors are, His forgiveness is ever-present. He invites you to draw near to Him (Matthew 11:28). The blood of Christ purifies you (1 John 1:7-9), and He will never abandon you (Hebrews 13:5). Will you embrace the love He offers?

Your Reflection

{ Were you ever taught to choose God before He chooses you?

{ Do you feel that God will turn his back on you if you're less than perfect?

{ How do you feel knowing you were chosen from the beginning?

{ How do you feel knowing that no matter what you do or how you feel about yourself, God still chooses you?

_____

_____

_____

_____

_____

_____

_____

~~Who Am I?~~ Who Does God Say I Am?

_____

_____

_____

_____

_____

_____

_____

_____

_____

_____

_____

2 Corinthians 6:18

And, "I will be a Father to you, and you will be my sons and

daughters, says the Lord Almighty."

John 1:12-13

Yet to all who did receive him, to those who believed in his name, he gave the right to become children of God—children born not of natural descent, nor of human decision or a husband's will, but born of God.

Breanna Williams

I Am A Child Of God

Growing up without a relationship with my dad, I missed important lessons that might have instilled confidence in me as a young woman. I am incredibly grateful for my amazing mom, but there were times when she didn't have the answers I sought.

In those moments when she couldn't fully understand my feelings or offer the support I needed, I often felt alone and disappointed. After all, isn't it natural to expect our parents to know us inside and out?

I recognize that God created both me and my parents. He gently reminds me that they have their own limitations and can only do so much. They, too, depend on Him for wisdom and understanding. I honor and cherish my mother and father deeply (Ephesians 6:2-3), and I hold the realization close to my heart that my Heavenly Father is always there to meet the needs my earthly parents may not be able to fulfill. This understanding brings me a profound sense of peace.

Your Reflection

{ Have you ever felt that your parents couldn't provide the support you needed?

{ Do you recognize that God is also guiding them?

{ Are you aware that they, like you, have their own limitations?

{ Reflect on how God was present in those solitary times.

{ Do you understand how He embodies both your mother and father?

_____

_____

_____

_____

_____

_____

Breanna Williams

~~Who Am I?~~ Who Does God Say I Am?

_____

_____

_____

_____

_____

_____

_____

_____

_____

_____

_____

John 15:5

I am the vine; you are the branches. If you remain in me and I in you, you will bear much fruit; apart from me you can do nothing.

I Am A Branch Of The True

Vine

Are you genuinely connected with Christ? Or are you bearing the weight of the world from your own strength?

Come to me, all you who are weary and burdened, and I will give you rest" (Matthew 11:28).

The main reason I became exhausted and spiritually drained is that I relied on my own power to get me through life. When all along, Christ was asking me to plug into Him, and He would give me His ultimate strength.

"I can do all this through him who gives me strength" (Philippians 4:13).

I finally realized that as long as I stay connected with Christ, I have more certainty, peace, and rest because I am using His strength, and He will not allow me to fail.

Your Reflection

{ What burdens are you bearing alone?

{ Why are you afraid to share your burdens with Christ?

{ Talk to Him about it.

_____

_____

_____

_____

_____

_____

_____

Breanna Williams

~~Who Am I?~~ Who Does God Say I Am?

_____

_____

_____

_____

_____

_____

_____

_____

_____

_____

_____

Breanna Williams

John 15:13-14

Greater love has no one than this: to lay down one's life for one's friends.

You are my friends if you do what I command.

I Am Jesus's Friend

Your friends have been with you through thick and thin and during the ups and downs. Your friends challenge you to do right and push you to be your best. Some friends have even taken the blame for you.

However, have any of them adored you so much that they gave their life for you?

Christ died in the most grueling and shameful way—death on the cross.

And all He asks of you is to obey His commands because He will tell you everything you need to know about God and yourself.

He asks you to listen to Him because He understands your feelings, your shame, your broken heart, and all your pain. He took it all and nailed it to the cross.

Christ is the plug.

Jesus answered, "I am the way and the truth and the life. No one comes to the Father except through me" (John 14:6).

Your Reflection

{ What is on your mind?

{ Do you have friends?

{ Do you need a friend?

{ What do you need in a friend?

{ Do you believe Christ can fulfill those needs?

{ Why or why not?

_____

_____

_____

_____

_____

~~Who Am I?~~ Who Does God Say I Am?

_____

_____

_____

_____

_____

_____

_____

_____

_____

_____

_____

_____

Breanna Williams

John 15:15-16

I no longer call you servants, because a servant does not know his master's business.

Instead, I have called you friends, for

everything that I learned from my Father I have made known to you.

You did not choose me, but I chose you and appointed you so that you might go and bear fruit—fruit that will last—and so that whatever you ask in my name the Father will give you.

I Am Not A Servant

You are not a servant of God.

He does not need you to serve Him in the traditional sense. He desires a relationship with you, a relationship built on love and understanding, not servitude.

Once again, you were chosen. Chosen to bear fruit: love, joy, patience, kindness, goodness, faithfulness, gentleness, and self-control (Galatians 5:22). Because these attributes serve you, they make you feel good and a better person.

Christ says so that you can ask the Father for anything.

If you were a parent—and maybe you are—you would want the best for your children, and you would want them to ask you for all they want. If their requests serve them, you will fulfill them, right?

The Father wants you to be His child, accept His love, and allow Him to care for you.

The same things you want for your children.

Your Reflection

❴ In what ways are you working to serve the Father?

❴ Do you feel you must prove your worth?

❴ Why do you feel that way?

❴ What do you want and need from God?

❴ Trust that He will provide.

_____

_____

_____

_____

_____

_____

Breanna Williams

~~Who Am I?~~ Who Does God Say I Am?

_____

_____

_____

_____

_____

_____

_____

_____

_____

_____

_____

Romans 3:23-24

For all have sinned and fall short of the glory of God, and all are justified freely by his grace through the redemption that came by Christ Jesus.

I Am Justified By His Grace

Mercy — Deserving punishment and not receiving it.

Grace — Deserving nothing, yet given a blessing.

Christ loved you so much that even though you did nothing to deserve it, He still gave His life for you to live a life free from shame, regret, guilt, and fear.

By HIS GRACE, you are redeemed.

By HIS GRACE, you are justified.

Your Reflection

{ Create a heartfelt list of the mistakes you have yet to forgive yourself for.

{ Reflect on what others have called you and the things they said about you. How did these comments shape your beliefs about yourself?

{ Consider the identity you adopted as a result.

{ As you revisit your list, gently remind yourself:

{ Yes, I made mistakes, but my Father loves me, so He has forgiven me and bestowed grace upon me.

I AM REDEEMED.

I AM JUSTIFIED.

~~Who Am I?~~ Who Does God Say I Am?

_____

_____

_____

_____

_____

_____

_____

_____

_____

_____

_____

_____

Breanna Williams

~~Who Am I?~~ Who Does God Say I Am?

_____

_____

_____

_____

_____

_____

_____

_____

_____

_____

_____

Romans 8:1-2

Therefore, there is now no condemnation for those who are in Christ Jesus, because through Christ Jesus the law of the Spirit who gives life has set you free from the law of sin and death.

I Am Not Condemned

In Christ Jesus, I am not condemned. Since I am not condemned in Him, I will stop condemning myself.

Is it time to begin the healing process and forgive yourself? To stop punishing yourself? Christ is not condemning you.

Your Reflection

{ The Father has given you GRACE.

{ The Father is not condemning you.

{ You are forgiven.

{ What must you forgive yourself for?

{ What are you still holding on to?

{ One step at a time, one piece at a time, will you place it on the altar and let it go?

_____

_____

_____

_____

_____

_____

~~Who Am I?~~ Who Does God Say I Am?

_____

_____

_____

_____

_____

_____

_____

_____

_____

_____

_____

_____

Breanna Williams

Romans 8:14-17

For those who are led by the Spirit of God are the children of God.

The Spirit you received does not make you slaves, so that you live in fear again; rather, the Spirit you received brought about your adoption to sonship. And by him we cry, "Abba, Father."

The Spirit himself testifies with our spirit that we are God's children.

Now if we are children, then we are heirs—heirs of God and co-heirs with Christ, if indeed we share in his sufferings in order that we may also share in his glory.

I Am A Child Of God.

I Am A Son Of God.

I Am A Daughter Of God.

I Am An Heir Of God.

You were adopted from the law of sin.

For Christ came to earth, put on your sin, nailed it to the cross, and said, "It is finished" (John 19:30).

Your adoption was sealed on the cross to become one with God, one with your father, "Abba" (Romans 8:15).

All God ever wanted to do was to be your dad and hang out with you. That is what He did with Adam and Eve in the Garden of Eden. It was just them and Father every day in harmony. And that is what the Father wants today with you through the Holy Spirit:

> The Spirit Comforts (John 14:16 KJV).

The Spirit Advocates (John 14:16 NIV).

The Spirit Discerns (John 14:17).

The Spirit Speaks (John 16:13).

The Spirit Guides (John 16:13).

Your Reflection

‹ You are a son of God.

‹ You are a daughter of God.

‹ You are not alone.

‹ The Father is not as far as you believe Him to be.

_____

_____

_____

_____

_____

_____

_____

~~Who Am I?~~ Who Does God Say I Am?

Breanna Williams

_____

_____

_____

_____

_____

_____

_____

_____

_____

_____

_____

2 Corinthians 5:17

Therefore, if anyone is in Christ, the new creation has come:

The old has gone, the new is here!

I Am A New Creation

The idea of starting anew, of letting go of the past and recognizing that it no longer defines you, can be a profound challenge for everyone, including yourself.

We often carry the belief that we must atone for our mistakes, that justice must prevail, and that we are responsible for mending our wrongs to create better outcomes.

But here's the truth: You are not that person anymore.

Once you accepted Christ, you became a new creation in His eyes.

Embrace this transformation! It's a beautiful gift of grace and renewal.

Your Reflection

{ What in your past are you holding on to?

{ How long have you been working to mend the broken pieces or prove to yourself and others you've changed?

{ What is it going to take to understand that nothing you do will end the love God has for you?

{ What will it take to live in the truth that your shortcomings – past, present, and future – have been nailed to the cross and forgiven?

{ What is one thing you can do today to step into the truth that you are a new person?

Breanna Williams

~~Who Am I?~~ Who Does God Say I Am?

_____

_____

_____

_____

_____

_____

_____

_____

_____

_____

_____

_____

Breanna Williams

_____

_____

_____

_____

_____

_____

_____

_____

_____

_____

_____

_____

1 Corinthians 15:56-58

The sting of death is sin, and the power of sin is the law.

But thanks be to God! He gives us the victory through our Lord Jesus Christ.

Therefore, my dear brothers and sisters, stand firm. Let nothing move you. Always give yourselves fully to the work of the Lord, because you know that your labor in the Lord is not in vain.

Breanna Williams

I Am Victorious

Christ has defeated death and given you victory over:

Sin

Shame

Guilt

Fear

Heartbreak

Disappointment

Temptation

Evil Spirits

Sickness

For God has not given us the spirit of fear; but of power, and of love, and of a sound mind (2 Timothy 1:7).

Your Reflection

{ What are you trying to overcome at this moment?

{ Do you feel powerless and defeated?

{ Are you trying to do it on your own, relying solely on your own strength?

{ Why?

{ *I can do all things through Christ who strengthens me (Philippians 4:13)*

{ Have you asked Christ for his strength?

{ Ask him now, and be ok with the help he provides, no matter the packaging.

Breanna Williams

_____

_____

_____

_____

_____

_____

_____

_____

_____

_____

_____

_____

~~Who Am I?~~ Who Does God Say I Am?

Breanna Williams

_____

_____

_____

_____

_____

_____

_____

_____

_____

_____

_____

_____

Romans 8:35-39

Who shall separate us from the love of Christ? Shall trouble or hardship or persecution or famine or nakedness or danger or sword?

As it is written: "For your sake we face death all day long; we are considered as sheep to be slaughtered."

No, in all these things we are more than conquerors through him who loved us.

For I am convinced that neither death nor life, neither angels nor demons, neither the present nor the future, nor any powers, neither height nor depth, nor anything else in all creation, will be able to separate us from the love of God that is in Christ Jesus our Lord

I Am More Than A Conqueror

No force can truly separate you from the love of God. Remember, no individual, evil entity, or challenging situation has the power to distance you from the nurturing love of your Father.

In times of hardship, when the weight feels overwhelming, cling to this promise. When it seems unbearable, lean into the assurance that through the love of Jesus, you have the strength to rise above and are more than a conqueror.

Your Reflection

❴ List the things, people, situations, hardships, and fears that worry you.

❴ Declare that through the love of Jesus, you conquer them all!

_____

_____

_____

_____

_____

_____

_____

Breanna Williams

~~Who Am I?~~ Who Does God Say I Am?

_____

_____

_____

_____

_____

_____

_____

_____

_____

_____

_____

Philippians 4:19

And my God will meet all your needs according to the riches

of his glory in Christ Jesus.

I Am Cared For

Everything you need, God has supplied it for you. Even the desires of your heart, all you have to do is ask the Father, and He will provide. Like any good parent, God wants to care for you.

If you believe, you will receive whatever you ask for in prayer (Matthew 21:22).

Ask and it will be given to you; seek and you will find; knock and the door will be opened to you (Matthew 7:7).

How much more will your Father in heaven give good gifts to those who ask him! (Matthew 7:11)

Your Reflection

﹛ The Father provides everything you need or want. All you have to do is accept it.

﹛ Is anything holding you back from accepting the Father's promises to you?

Revelation 22:21

The grace of the Lord Jesus be with God's people. Amen.

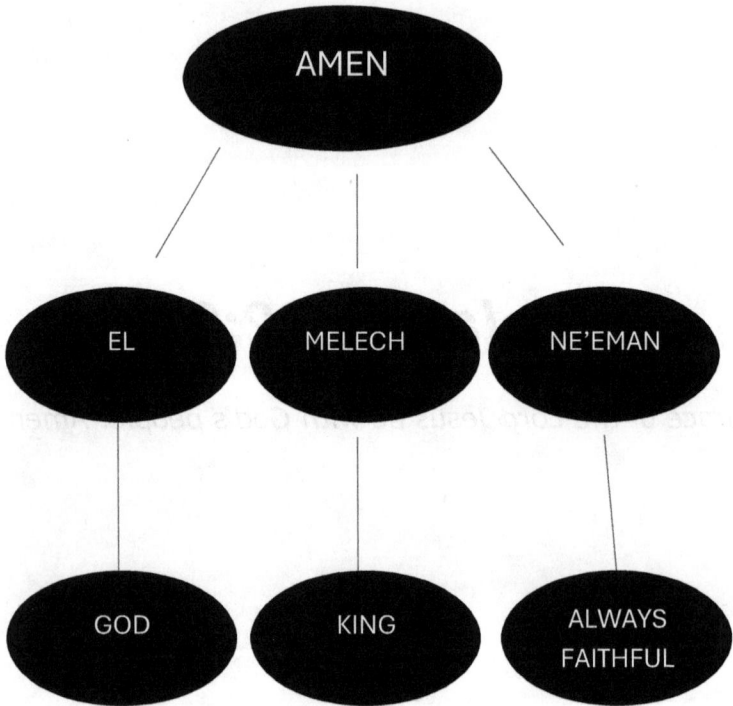

Alpha And Omega

The word "AMEN" isn't just a term we use; it carries deep roots in Hebrew, symbolizing something profound. For so long, I thought Amen merely indicated agreement in prayer, but it embodies a powerful declaration: "God is the King who provides and is unwavering in faith."

As I reflect on the countless ways God has blessed me, I find that my list keeps growing. There's a tangible fatigue that sets in as I write, yet the blessings continue to flood my mind.

His love for me shines through every trial, proving unceasingly that He is the father I need. Even in the absence of my biological father, I've always felt His presence nurturing and guiding us both.

In moments of doubt, He believes in me, even when I can't see the potential within myself. His love for me began long before I even existed.

From the start of the Bible to its conclusion, God is the cornerstone of everything.

God is Alpha—the beginning (Genesis 1:1).

God is Omega—the end (Revelation 22:13).

Understanding that He was present before my existence and will exist eternally brings me immense peace and assurance in embracing Him as my father.

Your Reflection

{ Everything you need or want, the Father provides it. All you have to do is accept it.

{ Is anything holding you back from accepting the Father's promises to you?

_____

_____

_____

_____

_____

_____

_____

Breanna Williams

~~Who Am I?~~ Who Does God Say I Am?

_____

_____

_____

_____

_____

_____

_____

_____

_____

_____

_____

_____

I AM A KING'S KID

Countless scriptures demonstrate the profound love story woven throughout the Bible, illustrating a Father's love for His children. As you travel on your journey as a King's Kid, take a moment to engage with the Father. Ask Him to reveal Himself to you in a way that feels clear and tangible, and observe how the scriptures resonate and appear in your own life.

He desires to spend quality moments with you, to care for you, and to shower you with love. It's about being connected with you, like a doting Daddy.

You are incredibly important to Him, so much so that He continues to bless you abundantly, regardless of whether you feel deserving of these gifts. Why does He do this? Simply because you are His son or daughter. You are a cherished child of the Most High, the Lord of Lords, and the King of Kings.

Since Father created you, the more you delve into learning about Him, the deeper your understanding of yourself becomes.

Remember, you are a King's Kid.

ABOUT THE AUTHOR

Breanna Williams is a 34-year-old Navy veteran, speaker, and passionate identity advocate. As the host of *The Anchored Identity Podcast*, she creates a safe space for women to confront their struggles, find healing, and anchor their identity in God. A proud Daughter of the King, Breanna knows firsthand the deep pain of an identity crisis. It was through her own journey of brokenness and restoration that her ministry was born.

While she draws from trusted tools and expert resources on healing and identity, Breanna's most powerful weapon is her personal experience—and the redemptive stories of others. Her heart beats to help others discover who they are in Christ and live from that truth with confidence and clarity. Whether through her podcast, writing, or one-on-one conversations, Breanna is on a mission to help others heal, grow, and thrive in their God-given identity.